Also by Robert Nye

Poetry
Juvenilia 1
Juvenilia 2
Darker Ends
Two Prayers
Agnus Dei
Five Dreams
Divisions on a Ground
A Collection of Poems 1955-1988
14 Poèmes
Henry James and Other Poems
Collected Poems
16 Poems
The Rain and the Glass: 99 Poems, New and Selected

Fiction
Doubtfire
Falstaff
Merlin
Faust
The Voyage of the Destiny
The Memoirs of Lord Byron
The Life and Death of My Lord Gilles de Rais
Mrs Shakespeare: The Complete Works
The Late Mr Shakespeare
Tales I Told My Mother
The Facts of Life and Other Fictions

As Editor
A Choice of Sir Walter Ralegh's Verse
William Barnes, Selected Poems
A Choice of Swinburne's Verse
The Faber Book of Sonnets
The English Sermon 1750-1850
PEN New Poetry 1
First Awakenings: The Early Poems of Laura Riding
A Selection of the Poems of Laura Riding
Some Poems by Ernest Dowson
Some Poems by Thomas Chatterton
Some Poems by Clere Parsons
The Liquid Rhinoceros and Other Uncollected Poems
by Martin Seymour-Smith
Some Poems by James Reeves

Robert Nye
An Almost Dancer
Poems 2005-2011

Robert Nye
An Almost Dancer
Poems 2005-2011

GREENWICH EXCHANGE

LONDON

Greenwich Exchange, London

First published in Great Britain in 2012
All rights reserved

An Almost Dancer © Robert Nye 2012

This book is sold subject to the conditions that it shall not, by way of trade or otherwise, be lent, resold, hired out or otherwise circulated without the publisher's prior consent in any form of binding or cover other than that in which it is published and without a similiar condition including this condition being imposed on the subsequent purchaser.

Printed and bound by imprintdigital.net
Cover design by December Publications
Tel: 028 90286559

Greenwich Exchange Website: www.greenex.co.uk

Cataloguing in Publication Data is available
from the British Library

ISBN: 978-1-906075-72-9 (hbk)
978-1-906075-39-2 (pbk)

To Warren Hope

CONTENTS

Foreword	*13*
Matches	*17*
Bicycling, with Birds	*18*
De Carne Christi	*19*
Valentinus	*20*
On the Sea-Wall	*21*
Mentchikoffs	*22*
Runes	*23*
Translation of an Unwritten Poem from the Greek Anthology	*26*
Gamblers	*27*
The Miracle at Cana	*28*
The Ghost of Chatterton	*30*
The Knock-Out	*31*
Father Hopkins Considers the Irishry	*32*
Menocchio's Crime	*33*
Drinking Hot Chocolate in the Rain	*35*
The Lady with the Dog	*36*
Lines to the Queen of Elsewhere	*37*
A Postcard from Crete	*38*
In Still Winter	*39*
An Apology for Rhetoric	*40*
At Delphi	*41*
A Word to the Wise, from Oscar	*42*
A Matador Past His Prime	*43*
The Apple Secret	*44*

An Almost Dancer	*45*
Conundrum	*46*
Going On	*47*
Gone Now	*48*
My Father's Tanks	*49*
Instructions for a Burial	*50*
Flights	*51*
First Love	*52*
Request	*53*

Foreword

It was my friend the American poet Warren Hope who first drew my attention to a very good remark made by Norman Cameron, to the effect that he wrote a poem because he thought that a poem wanted to be written. This surely puts the emphasis where it belongs – on the impulsion of the poem, rather than any compulsion in the poet. It implies also that patience could be one of the prime poetic virtues.

I invoke that saying now to apologise for the fact that what is offered here does not amount to much – a mere 33 poems as the work of the past seven years. So am I claiming that the poems in this book were all written because each one seemed to want to be written? More or less, yes, some of them more than others, of course, but in each case certain lines came into my head unbidden which then required resolving before they'd let me rest. I don't know any better way of putting it than Cameron's. But then I must admit that now in my seventy-third year the process of poetic composition is still as much a mystery to me as it ever was, perhaps more so. As for patience, possess it if you can. At all events, only a fool goes out and dances naked on the mountain-top in hope of being struck by lightning. The Muse may love her fools, but she also has a way of ignoring naked dancers.

Acknowledgement should be made to the editors of magazines where some of these poems first saw the light of day: *The Times Literary Supplement, PN Review, The London Magazine, The Dark Horse, The Spectator* and *The Shop: A Magazine of Poetry*. And I am again grateful to both the Royal Literary Fund and the Authors' Foundation for their patronage.

The poems are presented in what Martin Seymour-Smith once called their proper order, which (as most poets and many readers of poetry will know) is nearly, but never quite, chronological. I hope that none of the poems needs explication, but regarding the one remembering that fine poet I had better explain that we had this lifelong joke in which Martin ironically cast himself as Valentinus, the second-century Gnostic teacher, with me as his opponent Tertullian on account of my supposed orthodoxy.

Robert Nye
Kingsland
Co Cork

MATCHES

Some matchsticks in a patch of melting tar
Held my attention for perhaps an hour
One afternoon when I was rising four.
Crouched in the shadow of some willow trees
I stared at them and saw the way love sees,
And all was close and clear and singular.

Three matchsticks in a black hot patch of tar,
One spent, one bent, one still a fusilier
Standing up proud and perpendicular
With fire in his head, my cavalier.
Well, I knelt by them on my naked knees,
Transfixed as always by simplicities.

I loved those lordlings of the molten square,
My puny masters stuck in hot black tar,
Though only now I've worked the reason out
(If love needs reasons, which of course I doubt):
We're outcast in this world, and derelict,
Matches from nothing into nowhere flicked.

BICYCLING, WITH BIRDS

What I remember when I'd think of you
Who once possessed the power to stop my heart
Is how one summer morning we rode out
Down leafy lanes on new red bicycles
Not so much following a pair of birds
As being led by them.
                        Was it delight
That made those whitethroats dance upon the air?
They seemed to know where we would go before
We knew the way ourselves.
                                They flickered there,
Darting about our handlebars, our heads,
A pair of common birds, but magical,
Leading us on, and singing as they flew.

We rang our bells for them, and for the joy
Of being young, and bicycling, with birds.

DE CARNE CHRISTI

Tertullian, that brilliant man,
Believed because he knew
A story so impossible
Is certain to be true.

VALENTINUS
in memory of Martin Seymour-Smith

Yes, I knew Valentinus from my youth.
He taught me poets have to tell the truth
Or try to, though it make us seem uncouth.

You find this foolish? Lady, so did he,
Laughing at his own verses, teaching me
To laugh at mine or simply let them be.

Not that it's ever simple to make sense
At least when living in the present tense,
Or to be more than your intelligence.

Anyway, Valentinus was a man
Who knew a thing or two, and how to scan.
Let me recall his knowledge while I can.

He used when he was drunk sometimes to say
The heart is pure as the most perfect day,
Though sober he would speak another way.

Of that I shall not tell. But once (when I
On parting from him ran back suddenly
And shook his hand) it was my privity

To see tears in his eyes which certainly
Spoke of the heart's essential purity.
O my friend Valentinus, pray for me!

Now death has proved your poems not untrue
And there is nothing more that we can do,
Ah pray for me, dear foe, as I for you.

ON THE SEA-WALL

With Martin on the sea-wall
But knowing he was dead,
'Now you know more,' I said.

He did not shake his head
Nor did he nod assent,
Said 'You all right?' instead.

I thought of lying, didn't.
'Not really, no,' I said,
Half laughing and half crying,
Since I was only dying.

MENTCHIKOFFS

The special comforts of a Russian prince
Sold by a small shop in a cobbled street
Found seemingly by chance ... Do you recall
Those sweetmeats, almonds coated in burnt sugar,
Tasting like Fabergé made edible,
We gorged upon one afternoon at Chartres?

The shop stood in the shadow of that house
Which holds a fragment of the Virgin's dress.
The chocolatier was called Bazile.
The sweets were Mentchikoffs, Prince Mentchikof's
Secret confection, made to please the Tsar
And Catherine, who liked their bitterness.

You liked it too. And yet it was not bitter,
No, not exactly, more an aftertaste
Of sweets long gone, or foretaste of a sweet
Not yet perfected, tasting of itself
Yet sacramental, each one like a tear
Wept by an angel far away from home.

As for Our Lady's dress, we never saw it,
Being too satisfied with Mentchikoffs.
We came away with almond on our lips
And in our hearts a taste of homelessness.
All I have left now is this empty box
Which does not even smell of Mentchikoffs.

RUNES

'That boy is mad,' my uncle said.
   He'd followed me to school
And noted all the things I did
   Which proved I was a fool.

I'd walk seven strides, then run seven more,
   Then skip, and turn about
To kick the lamp-post with my boot,
   And give the wind a clout.

I'd stop outside the rabbi's house
   To pull up both my socks,
Then whirl seven times, and widdershins,
   Around the pillar-box.

There was a wall I had to touch,
   A drain I liked to poke
With a green stick plucked from the hedge;
   A tree-trunk that I'd stroke,

And sundry paving-stones I leapt
   While others I would stand
Entranced upon, my eyes tight shut,
   My satchel in my hand.

At last, then, when I reached the school
   Whose portals opened wide
I had to turn my back on it
   Before I passed inside.

All this and more my uncle saw
    And came and told my Dad.
'The boy's a fool,' he said. 'It's cruel,
    But probably he's mad.'

I promised I would try to mend
    My manners and my ways.
They watched to see what I would do
    And so for several days

I practised only in my head
    My little occult flights,
Waiting until, their interest dead,
    I could resume my rites.

But I had learned a lesson:
    To keep my antics small
So no one guessed their import
    Or noticed me at all.

I learned to hide my meanings
    And not betray the fact
That my whole life consisted of
    A single magic act.

So was I mad, as uncle said,
    Or just compulsion's fool?
Neither, for no neurotic god
    Compelled me to his rule,

Nor was it really madness, but
    A way to not go mad,
Some runes to make the world to rhyme
    With things inside my head.

It was the muse of poetry
   Who held me in her spell
And made me measure all my steps
   And dance for her as well.

Before I ever wrote a line
   I was her small liege-man.
Playing the fool on the way to school
   Is where my verse began.

TRANSLATION OF AN UNWRITTEN POEM FROM THE GREEK ANTHOLOGY

Weep if you must, hang cypress at your door,
But do not trouble Hades with your groans.
The dead are tearless, that is their delight.
Quench her hot ashes with the yellow wine.

GAMBLERS

The day my father died he made two bets.
We found the docket folded in his wallet.
Both horses lost. Thus my inheritance –
Not nothing, no, but this absurd small itch
To take the bloody bookies to the cleaners
Just once before I die. Just once, please God,
Not for the money, though that would be nice,
More in revenge of the long odds against us.

THE MIRACLE AT CANA

What's seldom said about the miracle
At Cana is that too much wine was made.
Consider, Jesus tells the waiting servants
To fill six pots with water, each pot holding
Two or three firkins, about twenty gallons.
The liquid then drawn out is found to be
Wine of choice vintage, and the bridegroom's praised
For keeping back the best stuff till the last.

But six huge pots, each holding twenty gallons,
Would make nine hundred pints (stronger than beer)
With sixty more for luck. Remember also
This wine is called for only when the guests
Have drunk the booze the bridegroom has provided,
So that presumably a merry time
Has been already had by everyone.
What need to drown in more wine than enough?

The reason, so some say, is Messianic.
The new age was to be an age of plenty
And Israel's saviour might well usher in
The good times with a great feast for his people.
What better place than Cana for its start
And at a wedding too? The world's a wedding
As we all know, some of us more than others,
And all like wine, some more than others of course.

And yet, it seems to me, an irritation
Shows in what Jesus answers when his mother,
Beside him, nags and worries at his sleeve:
'They have no wine.' 'Woman, what's that to me?'

Wasn't he fresh arrived in Galilee
From that Dead Sea encounter with the devil
Where starving from a fast he had been tempted
To turn stones into bread to feed himself?

'My hour is not yet come.' There, can't you see
The shrug with which the son has turned away,
Leaving his mother to instruct the waiters
To do whatever he might say they should?
Perhaps it was indifference, nothing more,
Turned water into wine that day at Cana,
Either divine indifference or just knowing
Water can taste like wine when you are drunk.

THE GHOST OF CHATTERTON

I've never seen the ghost of Chatterton
But sometimes I have smelt it, sharp as day:
A scent half smegma and half innocence
Like the stale-almond sweetness of the may.

THE KNOCK-OUT
Cowden Clarke on Keats

There he stands, tapping on the window-pane
With his small fingers, warm and capable,
Chattering about this prize-fight he has seen:

'Three punches – left, right, left – smack in the chops!
Rat-*tat*-tat, just like that! The champion drops.
But first he spins, eyes rolling, in a swoon
Of sweet obliteration ...
                            Lord, he fell!
But even as he's falling Jack Randall
Dances about and cracks him on the chin –
Rat-*tat*-tat, in a trice! Greased light-en-ing!'

His nightingale sings on of course, but I
Prefer remembering his commentary
On that young boxer's three quick punches, plain
Poetry as his fingers tap the pane.

FATHER HOPKINS
CONSIDERS THE IRISHRY

Beware of reasoning with the Mahoneys.
They'll say their bees are big as little ponies,
Then when you ask them how such things can be
Or how such bees could ever possibly
Fit into any beehive anywhere,
They'll flute their fingers on the silver air
And cry, 'Begob now, that's their own affair!'

MENOCCHIO'S CRIME

Let's hear it for Domenico Scandella,
Known better as Menocchio the miller,
Burnt by the Holy Roman Inquisition
One day in winter, AD 1600.
He perished in the Friuli where he'd lived
All of his life, being then sixty-eight,
A man who came to trial in a white cloak
And a white lambskin jacket and wool cap,
With in his pocket just a bit of cheese.

Menocchio had ground out for himself
A chaos theory, a theogony
Not unlike Hesiod's. He claimed a mess
Preceded genesis, and then a mass
Formed from that mess, as cheese is made from milk,
And in that cheese some worms appeared, the angels,
With there among them God, the worm of worms.
Glory come forth as light from putrefaction!
Chaos of chaos, cheese of very cheese!

Menocchio was no mere heretic
But a true miller. The inquisitors
Attest he persevered with obdurate heart,
Striving with his polluted mouth to bring
Again to life Origen's heresy
That Jews and Turks and pagans can be saved
Even while they persist in their untruth.
Nor did he much change tune upon strappado.
But worst was what he said about the cheese.

Menocchio's crime was that of any poet
Who dares think big in homely images.
The only cure for this is still well-known:
To be made clean by purgatorial flame
So that you may be one with the eternal.
Pray for him if you like, Domenico
Scandella, to his friends Menocchio,
But light the bonfire first and thus acquit him
For evermore, poor worm, to dine on cheese.

DRINKING HOT CHOCOLATE
IN THE RAIN

Drinking some hot dark chocolate through a hole
In a cardboard cup as the bright rain came down
I saw the market and the people in it
Glorified and transfigured utterly
As if they were the very dream of God.

The chocolate in my cup held some vanilla,
A little stick, a pod I licked just once
As I stood staring at that shining scene,
Knowing that I was in it but not of it.
My tongue went out to taste the raindrops then.

There in the market by that coffee-stall
I saw the world turned inside-out. The rain
Flew upwards like so many crystal sparks
Returning to the glory of the sun
As I drank my dark chocolate to the dregs.

This, this is ecstasy, to stand and drink
Hot chocolate in the rain, lost in a crowd
Of strangers, and to feel for them such love
As Dante felt for Beatrice when he saw
Her passing by and his own heart bowed down.

THE LADY WITH THE DOG

I saw a little old woman being led
Up a Cork alley by a mongrel dog.
The dog was wall-eyed and it had the mange
And slavered as it pulled her on a string,
Yet as they passed I heard the woman chant
In a low voice, as sweet as Juliet,
'Who is my joy? Who is my darling boy?
Wolfie, my dear, aren't you the dog of dogs!'
I hurried on, for I had things to do,
But when all's done I hope I shan't forget
That lady and her love for one fine dog.

LINES TO THE QUEEN OF ELSEWHERE

Remembering places where I've never been
I see you there in all of them, no ghost
But a grave girl in a bright yellow smock,
Heavily pregnant with our first-born son.

Dear, you were Queen of Elsewhere in those days
And I your servitor, fetching you drinks
Of fizzy sherbet in a tall green glass,
Or ginger beer with ice cream bobbing in it.

Now we lie far apart, yet I still see
The foaming glass, that yellow smock, and you
Taking my hand to feel the baby kick.

No doubt such more-than-memories come too quick
To those estranged, but why should I recall
Being in places I've not been at all?

A POSTCARD FROM CRETE
in memory of Giles Gordon, 1940-2003

'Icarus,' you say, 'was clearly misdirected,
Waving himself to death in the Aegean.
He should have striven for the moon instead.'

You wrote from Crete, the fifth time in twelve years
The family had stayed at Rethymnon.
'Far fewer Germans than usual, mercifully.'

Too hot to do much sight-seeing, you report,
But the children have been 'thrilled to be informed
That Zeus was born in a cave just down the road.'

'We're even giving Knossos a duck this time.
But wonderful flowers, vegetation, reading,
Food, wine, ouzo, raki … Love from Giles.'

I turn the postcard over, foolishly
Looking for you, white-suited, on the boats
Crowding the harbour. You're not there, of course.

You're here in your own words, each scribbled sentence,
As you were always present in your words,
Filling them with your wit and your despair

That words can never quite hold what we are.
Maybe you should have striven for the moon,
But striving for the sun you flew as far

As any other Icarus I've known.
I miss your laughter, Giles. This card from Crete
Seems now I look at it your last good joke.

IN STILL WINTER

Here, in still winter, suddenly
Shadow turns white to silver on the wall
And in an instant all the things I see
Melt into one thing, an original
And flowing intuition of such light
As makes an almost day of utmost night.

Now at the edge of consciousness
I could believe that more or less
Each babe that's born, from its first cry,
Is God demanding, 'Who am I?'
Though some men, dying, ask the same,
And cry to Christ for why they came.

AN APOLOGY FOR RHETORIC

Shadows make white turn silver on a wall.
That's what I saw, and all I should have said.
Forgive me if it's not original,
But call this line to mind when I am dead.

AT DELPHI

The only time I found myself at Delphi
I asked that ancient oracle a question
Not to be put in words, not then, not now.

The answer came as I turned round to see
A crippled woman clutching at the arm
Of a drunk man who matched his step to hers.

A WORD TO THE WISE, FROM OSCAR
*At the height of his fame, Oscar Wilde turned down
a dinner invitation from the Thirteen Club.*

The thirteen members of the Thirteen Club
Sit down to dine each Friday the Thirteenth.
They work their way through thirteen courses served
By thirteen cross-eyed waiters garbed in green,
Then rise and smash the mirrors. They are young
And scoff at superstition, yet in this
They pay too much attention to the thing
They say they most despise.

                              If you are asked,
Decline all invitations to their feast.
Thank them of course for honouring you, but
Point out your presence would disfigure them.
Oh yes, and don't forget, in signing off:
Tell them your lucky number is thirteen.

A MATADOR PAST HIS PRIME

Honour the fat and stumbling matador
Who having lost one shoe kicks off the other
And turns to face the bull in stockinged feet.

THE APPLE SECRET

Doctor
Carol
Manwell
taught me
this great
secret:

If you
take a
common
apple
and you
cut it
through the
middle
(side to
side and
not straight
down) you
will find
a star
inside
it.

    Halve
one now
and see
yourself.

AN ALMOST DANCER

Once, on a hill in Wales, one summer's day
I almost danced for what I thought was joy.

An hour or more I'd lain there on my back
Watching the clouds as I gazed dreaming up.

As I lay there I heard a skylark sing
A song so sweet it touched the edge of pain.

I dreamt my hair was one with all the leaves
And that my legs sent shoots into the earth.

Laughing awake, I lay there in the sun
And knew that there was nothing to be known.

Small wonder then that when I stood upright
I felt like dancing. Oh, I almost danced,

I almost danced for joy, I almost did.
But some do not, and there's an end of it.

One night no doubt I shall lie down for good
And when I do perhaps I'll dance at last.

Meanwhile I keep this memory of that day
I was an almost dancer, once, in Wales.

CONUNDRUM

When you sleep your lips grow childish
Yet no matter what I do
To wake them without waking you
They refuse to answer me.
Come, let's resume our colloquy
With the conundrum of a kiss.
Like this, my dear, like this.

GOING ON

One afternoon near Notre Dame
I watched a man negotiate
The crowded pavement, carrying
A pot of coffee in one hand
With in his other hand a cake.

I saw him passing through the throng
Like one protected, on his lips
A smile which said he made his way
Towards some little private room
Where he'd take his repast alone.

Now when I think I can't go on
What I remember is that man
With some small comforts in his hands
Passing along a crowded street
Towards a room all of his own.

GONE NOW

Six weeks since I saw them cut
The grass. As I write these words
The sun comes out for the first time
Where we were. Six weeks since
I saw them cut the grass.

There was a man and a woman
With the shears. I saw them work
In silence but together
As I went past. There was a man
And a woman with the shears.

As I write these words the sun comes out
For the first time. They are gone now
And the grass grows again
Where we were. As I write these words
The sun comes out for the first time.

I saw them work in silence
But together. As I went past
A man and a woman cut
The grass. I saw them work
In silence but together.

They are gone now, the man
And the woman. I saw them cut
The grass that has grown again
Where we were. They are gone now,
The man and the woman.

MY FATHER'S TANKS

My father made me little magic tanks
From cotton reels and bits of broken candle.
A rubber band sufficed to give each one
A clockwork engine which he'd wind up tight
To drive the thing (zig-zag) across the lino,
Armed with a stub of pencil for a gun.

Quite how they worked I never quite worked out
And none would go for more than a few seconds
But when I think of him I think of them
And how I liked it that he called them magic
And how I thought that they looked more like snails
Than tanks, although I never told him so.

INSTRUCTIONS FOR A BURIAL

Bury me in a rut on Clay Pit Hill
In a cardboard box to let the worms in quick
And with no ceremony save the rain
To wash away my sins if it's so inclined.

For preference I'd like a five-barred gate
With a six-barred shadow to stand guard above
The place where I lie rotting. But if not
Then a white stone will do, with nothing on it.

A few peewits as mourners would be good
But if they have some better thing to do
Then I forgive them, as I now forgive
All those who trespass against me and tramp
Over that queer grave where my corpse decays
Stuck in a rut on top of Clay Pit Hill.

FLIGHTS

I could step off this hill as easy as spit
And hang in the wind and rise up with it
And over the valley fly for a bit.

I was never a bird but in my breast-bone
A bird's heart beats sometimes when I am alone.
Whatever it is, it is not my own.

Whatever it is, it is not my own heart
But it bears me up speechless until I'm a part
Of the way of the wind, with a wild bird's art.

FIRST LOVE

Muriel Lawson,
You were my first love.

When I was just ten
I followed you home
From junior school
And then stood outside
Your house in the rain
Without doubt squinting
Up at the window
I thought must be yours
Because it was bright.

Until you came out
And said your father
Was not feeling well
And the sight of me
Standing there getting
Wetter and wetter
Was making him feel
A whole lot sicker
So please go away!

Muriel Lawson,
My very first love.

REQUEST

If you would be so good, tell me the way
To Pickle Herring Street. It used to be
Somewhere round here, I know it did, but now
I just can't find it for the life of me
And nothing else will do. It's where I lived
When I was nearly happy, years ago.
I beg you, sir, for the sweet love of Christ,
Tell me the way to Pickle Herring Street.

Some Comments on the poems of Robert Nye

'There are poets who start young, burn bright – and then continue burning. They stay alive. They do the business. They persist in being themselves, while literary movements rise and fall around them. Robert Nye is one such person.'
– Helena Nelson, *PN Review*

'A poet of ideas, for whom philosophical enquiry and lyric merge into a single enterprise.'
– John Burnside, *The Scotsman*

'At his best, his work wears a curious permanence.'
– Carol Ann Duffy, *The Guardian*

'His poems are of today, but his subjects and themes have been current in English poetry for five centuries, and in some instances they are as old as Christendom. This effect, the temporal suspended in the archetypal, leads this reviewer to the belief that Robert Nye is the inheritor and accomplished practitioner of a tradition that runs from Ralegh and Donne to Robert Graves.'
– James Aitchison, *The Dark Horse*

'This is a poet you know you can trust. You can hear the whisper – or sometimes the whoop – of his inspiration.'
– Rachel Campbell-Johnston, *The Times*

'Some of the best lyric poetry I've read for quite a long time.'
– Peter Porter, *BBC Radio Four*

'Not to be recited whilst shaving.'
— David Cameron, *Literary Review*

'One of the most interesting poets writing today, someone with a voice unlike that of any of his contemporaries.'
— Gabriel Josipovici, *PN Review*

'He is, in short, a real poet.'
— Iain Crichton Smith